NOW YOU CAN READ....
THE FALL OF JERICHO

STORY RETOLD BY LEONARD MATTHEWS

ILLUSTRATION BY BERNARD LONG

Published by Rourke Publications, Inc., P.O. Box 3328, Vero Beach, Florida 32964. Copyright © 1984 by Rourke Publications, Inc. All copyrights reserved. No part of this book may be reproduced in any form without written permission from the publisher. Printed in the United States of America.

The Publishers acknowledge permission from Brimax Books for the use of the name "Now You Can Read" and "Large Type For First Readers" which identify Brimax Now You Can Read series.

Library of Congress Cataloging in Publication Data

Matthews, Leonard.
  The fall of Jericho.

  (Now you can read—Bible stories)
  Summary: Retells the Old Testament story about how Joshua caused the fall of the city of Jericho.
  1. Bible stories, English—O.T.   Joshua.
2. Jericho—Juvenile literature.   I. Title.   II. Series.
BS551.2.M368   1984   222'.209505   84-15904
ISBN 0-86625-304-1

GROLIER ENTERPRISES CORP.

NOW YOU CAN READ. . . .

THE FALL OF JERICHO

For many years, the people of Israel
lived and worked as slaves in Egypt.
A leader named Moses saved them.
He led them out of Egypt.
God had promised the people of Israel
that they would return to their home
in Canaan. Canaan lay to the east
of Egypt. They would have to travel
a long way to reach this promised
land. They were led first by Moses,
then by a wise man named Joshua.

For forty years Moses led the people of Israel through many lands. Moses died before they could reach Canaan. His place was taken by Joshua. To reach Canaan, the people would have to cross the River Jordan.

After crossing the River Jordan, they would have to capture the city of Jericho. Jericho was in Canaan. The people who lived there were enemies of the people of Israel. They would fight hard to defend their city, which was surrounded by strong walls. When Joshua and his people reached the river, Joshua made his plans. He sent two men to swim across the river and find a way into the city. "Find out all you can about the city and come back quickly," said Joshua.

Nobody saw the men as they slipped into the city at night. They wandered around, taking care not to be seen by any of the soldiers of the king of Jericho. It did not take them long to see that it would not be easy for Joshua and his army to capture Israel. They happened to meet a woman named Rahab. She let them stay in her house.

Rahab believed in the God of Israel.

"God gave this land to the people of Israel," she said. "I will help you."

The king of Jericho learned about the two men in Rahab's house. He sent  soldiers to capture them. Rahab heard that the soldiers were coming. She hid the two men on the roof of her house. Then she waited for the soldiers to arrive.

When the soldiers came, Rahab said, "The two men have left my house. I do not know who they were." The soldiers went back to the king.

That night, Rahab went up to the roof. She took a red rope with her.

The two men were waiting for her. "Climb down this rope to the street," she said. "Leave the city as quickly as you can."

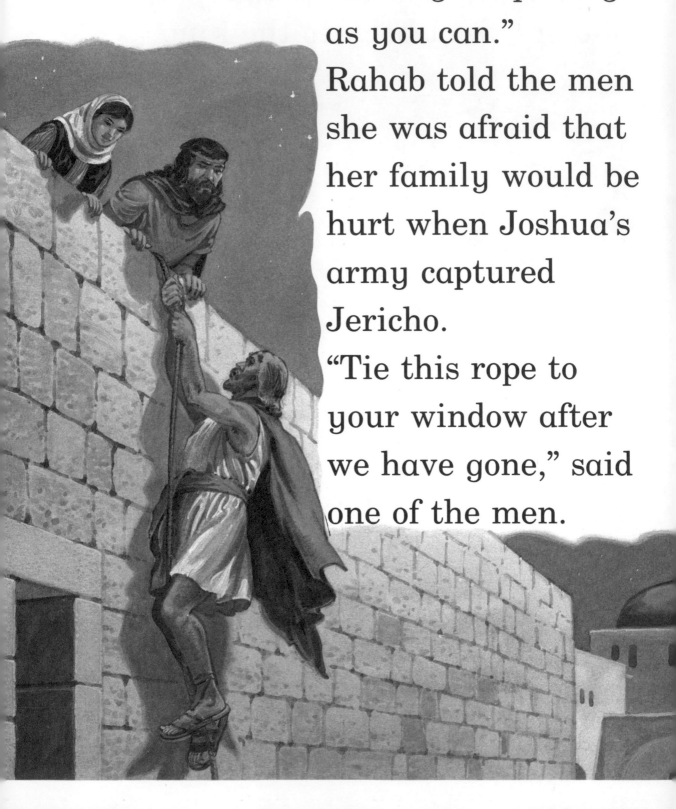

Rahab told the men she was afraid that her family would be hurt when Joshua's army captured Jericho.

"Tie this rope to your window after we have gone," said one of the men.

"We will tell Joshua about the red rope," said the other man. "No man of Israel will harm your house and family."

The two men slipped to the ground. They managed to get out of the city in the darkness. They went back to Joshua. "Many of us will be killed if we attack that city," they told Joshua.

"First," said Joshua, "we must cross the River Jordan. Then we will think about the city."

God had spoken to Joshua. He told him how the people of Israel could cross the river. Joshua gave the order to march forward. The priests led the way. They carried the golden Ark.

The Ark was a large box with two flat stones inside it. The Ten Commandments were carved on the stones. The people of Israel came to the river. Joshua said to the priests, "Walk across the river."

The water was deep. The priests stepped forward. Then something wonderful happened. The river stopped flowing. The river bed dried up. There was no water in the river.

"It is God's work," said Joshua. All the people crossed to the other side.

They took all their food, their sheep and cattle and everything they owned with them. As soon as everyone had crossed, the water started to flow again.

The people praised God. Joshua and
his people marched a long way to
Jericho. They stood looking at the
strong walls of the city.

"There is no chance of breaking through those stone walls," said one of Joshua's men. "It would be foolish to try and attack that city."

Joshua smiled when he saw that his men were afraid. "Do not be afraid," he said. "God has told me what to do. The women and children will stay here in camp. All the men will follow me. Seven priests must march with us."

Joshua said, "Each priest will
carry a trumpet. Four other priests
will carry the Ark behind us."
Then Joshua rode forward.

Every day for six days the army marched once around the city. The priests blew their trumpets. The seventh day was different. That day, the army marched around the city seven times. Then Joshua cried out, "Now shout!"

Everyone shouted. The walls of
Jericho fell down with a crash.
The people of Israel rushed into
the city. As promised, Rahab and her
family were not harmed. Now
the people of Israel could go home.

All these appear in the pages of the story. Can you find them?

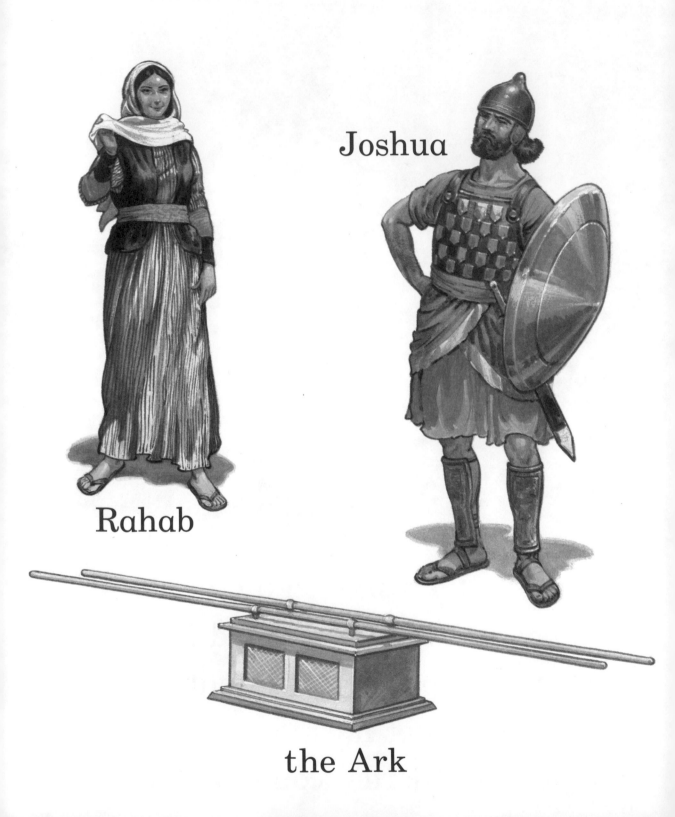

Joshua

Rahab

the Ark

Joshua's two men

priest

Jericho

Now tell the story in your own words.